CAMILLA
- AN UNTOLD STORY"

Her rise to Britain's Queen Consort

by Clive Wilcon

PREFACE

Prince Charles and Camilla Parker Bowles are celebrating their 14th anniversary, and hats off to them both. Prince Charles's reputation was severely tested by the divorce and death of Lady Diana Spencer. In the British Kingdom, Charles and Camilla are called "star-crossed lovers," the unfortunate lovers, an expression from Romeo and Juliet. Lady Diana had already known everything before the wedding and had revealed to her sister, "I cannot marry him."

Many years later, Lady Diana will reveal that July 29, 1981, was the worst day of her life. Camilla Shand had been considered unsuitable for the role of the wife of a future King because she had already had sexual experiences. Today, the bride's virginity is considered sexist and would not be very important. The Crown made all the gestures necessary to separate them. Camilla eventually accepted her fate, and her dream of love with Charles was shattered. Before choosing Diana, Charles dated other women for almost seven years. The first is Lucia Santa Cruz, the daughter of the Chilean ambassador, whom he had already known for some time. Why didn't Charles marry her? Because she was a Catholic, the heir to the throne must marry a Protestant. The same problem arose with American and Catholic Laura Watkins.

What went wrong with Davina Sheffield, granddaughter of the first Lord McGowan, perhaps the most beautiful flame of Charles? Charles dated model Fiona Watson for a short time: it quickly turned out that she had posed naked for Penthouse. Ditto, Sabrina Guinness was guilty of liaising with Mick Jagger, David Bowie, Rod Stewart, and Jack

Nicholson. Charles even went so far as to ask for the hand of a cousin, Amanda Knatchbull, who refused the offer for obvious reasons. Camilla first met Charles in the 1970s. Charles proposed to Diana in February 1981, and five months later, they were on the altar exchanging vows. In 1986 Charles and Camilla were already intimate again. Sources close to Camilla say that she was fascinated by the figure of her great-great-grandmother, the King's lover, and she thought she was carrying on her tradition. Camilla remained a thorn in the side of the Mountbatten-Windsor family.

The separation between Charles and Diana is announced and in 1995, the couple of the century divorced due to the classic incompatibility of character. A year after Diana's death and a year of mourning, Charles introduces Camilla to his children, William and Harry. Queen Elizabeth holds out; she doesn't even attend Charles's 50th birthday party. Camilla seems to be made of rubber, you can throw any problem at her, and it bounces off her. The following year, Charles and Camilla share their first kiss in public. In 2003 Camilla moved "to Charles's home." Too mature to play kids, people have nothing to object to if they live together at Clarence House. When they announced their engagement in 2005, some objections were raised. In the end, it is decided to let them join in marriage two months later. So, let's dive into the life and journey of Camilla (The Duchess of Cornwall) and how she rose to the Queen Consort against all odds.

Table of Contents

CAMILLA ROSEMARY, DUCHESS OF CORNWALL

INTRODUCTION

Camilla, The Former Duchess of Cornwall and now Queen Consort (born 17 July 1947 as Camilla Rosemary Shand, later Parker Bowles) is a member of the British Royal Family. She was also the Duchess of Rothesay and Countess of Chester. She was legally Princess of Wales, but she was given the title Duchess of Cornwall to honor Lady Di.

Camilla is the eldest daughter of Major Bruce Shand and Rosalind Cubitt, the daughter of Roland Cubitt, third Baron Ashcombe. She was brought up in East Sussex and South Kensington, England, and received her education in England, Switzerland, and France. Camilla married British

Army officer Andrew Parker Bowles in 1973 and had two children. In 1995, they separated and got divorced.

Camilla later became the 2nd wife of Charles (Prince of Wales, the British heir apparent, and now the King of the United Kingdom of Great Britain and Northern Ireland). They got married on April 9, 2005 (their second marriage). Despite having the right to be known as the Princess of Wales, she preferred the title Duchess of Cornwall, her husband's secondary title. She was popularly referred to as the Duchess of Rothesay in Scotland.

Moreso, Camilla had a romantic relationship with the Prince of Wales before and during his first marriage. The relationship was widely publicized in the media and drew international attention. It culminated in 2005 with a civil marriage at Windsor Guildhall, followed by a televised Anglican blessing at St George's Chapel, Windsor Castle.

As Duchess of Cornwall, Camilla helped the Prince of Wales with his official duties. She is also a patron, president, and member of several charities and organizations. Since 1994, Camilla has acted on osteoporosis, earning honors and awards. She has raised awareness of rape and sexual abuse, literacy, animal welfare, and poverty. In her youth, Camilla studied French and French literature in Paris and worked as a secretary and decorator. She committed most of her free time to horseback riding and gardening.

Childhood And Education

Camilla Rosemary Shand was born at King's College Hospital in London on July 17, 1947. She grew up in the Lines, an 18th-century country house in Plumpton, East Sussex, and her family's second home, a three-story house in South Kensington.

Major Bruce Shand (1917-2006), a British Army officer-turned-businessman, and his wife, Rosalind (née Cubitt; 1921-1994), were her parents. Annabel Elliot is her younger sister, and Mark Shand is her younger brother (1951–2014). From 1898 to 1910, her maternal grandmother, Alice Keppel, was the mistress of King Edward VII. Camilla was baptized on November 1, 1947, at Fairley Church in East Sussex. Camilla's mother was a stay-at-home mom, and her father had a variety of business ventures after retiring from the military. He was a partner, most notably at Block, Gray, and Block, a wine merchant in Mayfair's South Audley Street, before joining Ellis, Son, and Vidler of Hastings and London.

Camilla became an avid reader as a child due to her father often reading to her. She grew up with dogs and cats and, at an early age, learned to ride a pony. She then joined Pony Club camps and won rosettes at the community gymkhana. According to Camilla, her childhood was "perfect in every way." Biographer Giles Brandreth describes her background and childhood:

Camilla is often described as having "a childhood like Enid Blyton." It was much more impressive than that. Camilla, at a very young age, may have had some of George's tomboy personality traits, but Enid Blyton's children were essentially middle-class kids, and The Shands were, without question, upper-class. The Shands had status, and they had help - in the house. Help, with the garden, help, with the kids. He was a gentleman. He opened his garden for the local Conservative Party Association's summer festival.

Camilla was sent to a co-educational school in Ditchling Village at age five. She left Dumbrels at age ten to attend Queen's Gate School in South Kensington. Her Queen's Gate classmates knew her as "Mila." Among her classmates was the singer Twinkle, who stated Camilla was a girl of "inner strength," free of "magnetism and self-confidence." Penelope Fitzgerald, a writer who taught French at the school, remembered Camilla as "bright and lively." Camilla graduated from Queen's Gate in 1964 with an O-Level; her parents did not allow her to stay for A-levels. When she was 16, she went to Mon Fertile, a finishing school in Tolochenaz, Switzerland. After finishing her course in Switzerland, she went to France for six months to study

French and French literature at the University of London Institute in Paris.

Camilla made her London debut on March 25, 1965, one of 311 students that year. She moved into a small flat in Kensington with her friend Jane Wyndham, the niece of decorator Nancy Lancaster. She later moved to Belgravia, where she shared a larger flat with her landlady, Lady Moira Campbell, daughter of the Duke of Abercorn, and then with Virginia Carrington, daughter of politician Peter Carrington, 6th Baron Carrington. From 1973 to 1979, Virginia already married Camilla's uncle Henry Cubitt (and became a special ally of Camilla and Prince Charles in 2005). Camilla worked as a secretary in the West End before being hired as a receptionist in Mayfair by the decorating firm Sybil Colfax and John Fowler. She passionately continued her passion for equestrian sports and often participated in equestrian activities. She also had a passion for painting, which eventually led her to take private tutoring with an artist, although most of her work "ended up in the bin." Other interests were fishing, gardening, and horticulture.

What was Camilla Parker Bowles like as a young woman?
From her youth to the present day, Camilla Parker Bowles has remained in the spotlight of the British press. With countless public appearances since her marriage to Andrew Parker Bowles, the now Queen consort has been, for years and long before her marriage to the now King of Great Britain, a constant in the public life of the kingdom. She started from a young age to join social causes in the United Kingdom, mainly the National Osteoporosis Society, in 1994, the same one she approached after her mother's death from the disease.

Weddings and Children

• First Marriage

Camilla met Andrew Parker Bowles (a Guards officer and Blues and Royals Lieutenant) in the late 1960s through her younger brother, Simon Parker Bowles, who worked in Mayfair for her father's wine firm. Andrew and Camilla announced their engagement in The Times in 1973 and married on July 4, 1973, in a Roman Catholic ceremony at Guards Chapel, Wellington Barracks in London. Parker Bowles was 33 years old, and Camilla was 25.

The Queen Consort, Camilla has two children (a son and a daughter) from her first marriage:

- Tom Parker Bowles (1974 p.),
- Laura Lopez (1978 p.)

  Camilla has 5 grandchildren
- Tom - Freddy (2010) and Lola (2007).
- Laura - Eliza (2008)
- Gus and Louis - Twins (2009).

Charles and Diana had two sons, whom the Queen Consort is now a stepmother:
- Prince William is now The Prince of Wales (1982 p.).
- Prince Harry (Henry) (1984 p.)

Bolehide Manor in Allington, Wiltshire

The couple settled in Wiltshire, buying Bolehyde Manor in Allington and then Middlewick House in Corsham. They had two children: Tom, Prince Charles' godson (born 1974), and Laura (born 1978). Both children were raised in their father's Roman Catholic faith. On the other hand, Camilla remained an Anglican and did not convert to Roman Catholicism. Laura went to a Catholic girls' school but married in an Anglican church, and Tom, unlike his father, did not attend Ampleforth College but married outside of Eton and the Catholic Church. Tom remained in the Earldom of Macclesfield, as did his father.

Camilla and her husband divorced in December 1994, after 21 years of marriage, because they had been living separately for years. Rosalind, her mother, died of osteoporosis in July of the same year, and her father later described it as a "tough time for her." In January 1995, the High Court Family Division in London heard and accepted their divorce petition. In March 1995, the divorce was finalized. Andrew Parker Bowles remarried Rosemary Pittman a year later (who died in 2010).

Relationship with Prince Charles

Camilla and Prince Charles allegedly met in the middle of 1971. Camilla and Charles shared a social circle and occasionally attended the same events, but they never met formally. Her biographer, Brandreth, states that the couple did not meet for the first time at a polo match, as is commonly believed. Instead, they met for the first time at the home of their friend Lucia Santa Cruz, who formally introduced them. They became close friends and eventually began to see each other, which was well-known in their social circle. They frequently met at polo matches at Smith's Lawn in Windsor Great Park, where Charles frequently played polo. He also appeared in Annabel's set in Berkeley Square. As their relationship progressed, Charles met Camilla's family in Plumpton, and he introduced her to some of his family members. After Charles traveled abroad to join the Royal Navy in early 1973, the relationship was put on hold and ended abruptly.

There have been several theories about why the couple's relationship terminated in 1973. In his 2008 book, Royal: Her Majesty Queen Elizabeth II, Robert Lacey stated that Charles met Camilla quite early and advised her not to wait. He was called to military duty in another country. In her 2007 book, Diana, Sarah Bradford stated that a member of Charles' great-granduncle Lord Mountbatten's intimate circle believed Mountbatten stopped their connection to make room for Charles' engagement. Charles's trip to Europe had been planned. According to some sources, Queen Elizabeth the Queen Mother did not accept the marriage because she wanted Charles to marry one of the Spencer family's daughters who would have been the granddaughters of her close friend Lady Fermoy. Other sources also suggest that Camilla did not wish to marry Charles, but rather to marry Andrew Parker Bowles as she had an affair with Parker Bowles that began in the late 1960s Or Charles had decided not to marry until he was thirty.

Most royal biographers agree that it would have been denied even if Charles and Camilla wanted to marry or tried for approval. According to some palace courtiers of that time, Camilla was deemed unsuitable to be the wife of the future King. One Palace insider stated, "Ultimately, you could say that Charles should have married Camilla when he first got the chance. They were ideally suited, we know now. But that was not possible." "It could not have happened then."

Nevertheless, they both stayed friends. In August 1979, Lord Mountbatten was assassinated by the Irish Republican Army terror group better known as the IRA. Charles was saddened by his death and relied heavily on Camilla for consolation. During this period, rumors began to spread among close friends of Parker Bowles and the polo-playing communities that Charles and Camilla had rekindled their intimate relationship. A source close to Camilla confirmed that by 1980 they had rekindled as lovers. The royal servants also claim that this happened earlier. Reportedly, Camilla's husband accepted the affair, who was said to have had several lovers during their marriage. In 1981, Charles married Lady Diana Spencer.

The affair between Charles and Camilla became public in the press a decade later, with the 1992 publication of Diana: Her True Story, followed by the 1993 Camillagate tape scandal, in which Camilla and Charles secretly had an intimate telephone conversation. The recordings were published in magazines. The book and tape immediately damaged Charles' public image. Meanwhile, Camilla was condemned by the media. In a televised interview with Jonathan Dimbleby in 1994. Charles eventually spoke about his relationship with Camilla. "Mrs. Parker Bowles is a very good friend of mine," he told Dimbleby during the interview...a friend for a long time. She will be a friend for a long time." He later admitted in interviews that the relationship between himself and Camilla was rekindled in 1986 after his marriage to Diana "unexpectedly broke."

What were Camilla Parker Bowles and Princess Diana's Relationships like?

The complicated love triangle between then Prince Charles, Camilla Parker Bowles, and Lady Di, was more complex than can ever be related. Between rumors and harassment by the press overturned by the charm of Diana Spencer, it marked, from a distance, a conflictive relationship between the three. However, the biography of the Duchess of Cornwall, *The Duchess: Camilla Parker Bowles and the Love Affair that Rocked the Crown*, recounts, when Lady Di began her relationship with Charles, she often visited Camilla., who was still married to Andrew. Diana was 19, and Camilla was 14 years older both at the time seeming, as confidants looking to find a way for the relationship between the heir to the throne and Lady Di to work.

However, after the engagement between Charles III and Diana Spencer, suspicions about an affair between the Prince and Camilla began to resonate, detailed in the biography that the prince's gifts to Camilla were constant. Highlighting one bracelet with an engraving with the initials G and F, Gladys and Fred, the nickname of the couple. Later, and according to Diana's biography, the suspicion would continue, especially when Diana found a photo of Camilla in Charles' diary on their honeymoon.

Charles And Diana: A Timeline of Their Relationship, From the First Date to the Scandal of Their Divorce

How did the romance start, and how did things get out of control between the couple, whose divorce was finalized in 1996?

Timeline:
November 1977

Prince Charles and Lady Diana Spencer first met at Althorp House, her family estate in Northamptonshire, England. She was 16 at the time; he was 28 at the time. Charles was dating Diana's older sister, Sarah, and was visiting her for a pheasant-hunting weekend.

"As Diana recalls, they met in the middle of a plowed field,'" according to a July 1981 article in The Daily Times. In an interview in 1981, Prince Charles remembered meeting Diana for the first time and described her as "a cheerful, fun, and attractive 16-year-old girl" who was "very funny, lively, and full of life."

Diana recalled their first meeting on private tapes published as a part of the 2017 documentary Diana: In Her Own Words, saying she was "astonished" to receive Prince Charles' attention when she was 16. "How could someone like that be interested in me?" she continued. Diana was dressed as a tree for a school production when they first meet inside Althorp House.

July 1980
In July 1980, Charles, who had recently broken up with Diana's sister (she married Neil Edmund McCorquodale that year), and Diana spent the weekend with a mutual friend, Philip de Pass, at his family's home in Sussex.
While there, Diana spoke to Charles about the murder of his great-uncle, Lord Mountbatten, with whom he had been very close. "The next minute, he jumped on me, practically," she said in the tapes released on Diana: In Her Own Words. "But then it built from there," she added of their courtship.

September 1980
Diana is photographed at the royal family's private estate in Scotland, Balmoral. The news of their relationship is widely publicized. Charles was hesitant to invite Diana, preferring Camilla Parker-Bowles to join him. He goes ahead after Parker-Bowles turns him down and encourages him to invite Diana. Charles invited Diana and she passes what royal insiders refer to as "the Balmoral test" for guests of the royal family.

February 1981

Prince Charles proposed to Diana at Windsor Castle in February 1981. Diana, 19, moved from Earl's Court to Clarence House to live with Charles. On February 24, the couple's engagement was formally announced. When a journalist asked Charles if the couple was in love, he replied, "whatever that means."

Charles calls the Queen to inform her that he has proposed to her. The Queen then informs the rest of the royal family. Charles claims he proposed to her in kindergarten without getting down on one knee. Diana, he claims, told him it was the happiest time of her life. Diana returns to London after the proposal and celebrates her engagement with friends at a nightclub. The Queen also shows her a selection of engagement rings, and she selects one that has not been passed down through the family and must be purchased. Diana also discusses Charles' line "whatever love means" with her friends.

March 1981

Charles is leaving for Australia and New Zealand for five weeks, and Diana is seen crying at Heathrow Airport. In Diana: In Her Own Words, the princess was quoted as saying, "It just broke my heart." While Charles is away, Charles does not call her for three weeks. Diana also has her first meeting with Camilla Parker-Bowles after Charles encourages them to spend time together. Diana learns Charles and Camilla's nicknames for each other: Fred and Gladys.

July 1981

The couple tied the knot after less than a year of dating in a luxurious ceremony at Westminster Abbey on July 29. An estimated 750 million people watched the event on television, and Diana was named Princess of Wales. Diana wears a dress designed by Elizabeth and David Emanuel. Diana had second thoughts about the wedding after discovering that Charles had bought Camilla a bracelet with the words "Fred & Gladys" engraved on it, but still went ahead with the wedding.

June 1982

The couple welcomes their first child together: Prince William. Diana suffered from postpartum depression after giving birth. Diana spoke about it to the BBC's Martin Bashir in 1995: "You woke up in the morning feeling like you didn't want to get out of bed; you felt misunderstood and very, very depressed about yourself."

March 1983

Charles and Diana go on a formal tour to Australia with Prince William. They are photographed looking happy and very much in love. Diana and Charles argue a lot on this trip, mainly because Diana has found secret letters from Charles to Camilla.

1986

According to his official biographer Jonathan Dimbleby, Prince Charles begins an affair with Camilla Parker-Bowles. It is reported that Diana's affair with Army Captain James Hewitt also starts at this time. Charles begins to see Camilla more often during this period.

1987
Diana stays home while Charles attends the royal family's annual summer vacation to Balmoral. This leads to speculation that the couple is splitting up for a while due to marital problems.

May 1992
Andrew Morton publishes details of Charles' affair with Parker Bowles in Diana: Her True Story. The princess secretly helped with the book, as it is now known that she supplied Morton with audio recordings.

November 1992
Charles and Diana visit South Korea on an official trip together and are called "the Glums" by the tabloids because they seem so unhappy.

December 1992
Then Prime Minister John Major announced that Charles and Diana were separating. "This decision was made amicably, and they will continue to be fully involved in raising their children," Major said in a statement from Buckingham Palace. Diana expressed "deep, deep, deep sadness" about the decision to divorce in a 1995 interview with the BBC's Panorama." "We had struggled to keep it going, but obviously, we had both run out of steam," she added.

August 1996
The divorce is finalized, and Diana relinquishes her status as Her Royal Highness. During a vacation with her sons, Princes William and Harry, Diana is photographed at the estate of

Mohammad Al-Fayed (whose son, Dodi Fayed, she was dating at the time).

August 1997

Diana is killed in a car accident in a road tunnel in Paris. Her partner, film producer Dodi Fayed, was also killed in the accident along with the couple's driver, Henri Paul.

In 2005, Prince Charles married Camilla Parker Bowles.

Image Rehabilitation

Following both divorces, Prince Charles stated that his relationship with Camilla was and continues to be "non-negotiable." Charles was aware that the relationship was generating much negative press, so he hired Mark Bolland, whom he had hired in 1995, to help him rebuild his image, to raise Camilla's public profile. Camilla served as Charles' unofficial partner at events on occasion. The couple made their first appearance in 1999 at the Ritz Hotel in London, where they went to a birthday party; nearly 200 photographers and reporters worldwide were present to witness them together. She accompanied Charles to Scotland for a series of official engagements in 2000, and in 2001, she became president of the National Osteoporosis Society, which presented her to the public for the first time.

Camila later met the Queen of England for the first time since the relationship was made known to everyone in 2000 at the 60th birthday party of Greece's former King, Constantine II. This meeting was interpreted as the Queen's approval of Charles and Camilla's relationship. After public and private appearances, Camilla was invited to the Queen's Golden Jubilee celebrations in 2002. She sat in the royal box behind the Queen during one of the Buckingham Palace concerts. Camilla kept her home, Ray Mill House, near Lacock in Wiltshire, which she purchased in 1995, but she moved to Clarence House, Charles' home and official residence, in 2003. Camilla accompanied Charles to almost all his official events in 2004, including a high-profile visit to Scotland's annual Highland Games. The media speculated on when they would declare their engagement, and polls in the UK showed widespread support for the marriage over time.

The Second Marriage

On February 10, 2005, Clarence House announced the engagement of Camilla and the Prince of Wales. Charles gave Camilla a diamond ring that is thought to have been given to her grandmother, Queen Elizabeth the Queen Mother when she gave birth to her daughter, Queen Elizabeth II, an engagement ring with a square-cut diamond on each side. Charles' marriage to a divorcee was controversial as the succeeding Supreme Governor of the Church of England, but the Queen, the government, and the Church of England all approved. The Queen, Archbishop of Canterbury Rowan Williams, and Prime Minister Tony Blair used their best wishes in media statements.

The wedding was supposed to take place on April 8, 2005, in a civil ceremony at Windsor Castle, followed by a religious service. To hold a civil marriage at Windsor Castle, however, the venue would need to obtain a civil marriage license, which it did not have. The site was shifted to the Town Hall at Windsor Guildhall because the royal family did not wish to open Windsor Castle to the public for legal weddings. The wedding was delayed by one day on April 4 to allow the

Prince of Wales and other invited dignitaries to attend Pope John Paul II's burial.

Charles and Camilla's parents did not attend the civil wedding; instead, Camilla's son Tom and Charles' son Prince William served as witnesses. The blessing service was attended by the Queen and the Duke of Edinburgh. The Queen later hosted a reception at Windsor Castle for the newlyweds. Among the performers were the St George's Chapel Choir, Welsh composer Alun Hoddinott, and the Philharmonia Orchestra. Ekaterina Semenchuk, a Russian mezzo-soprano singer, was sent to the UK as a wedding gift by the Mariinsky Theater Trust to perform a special song for the duet. Following the wedding, the couple traveled to the prince's Scottish country home, Birkhall, where they performed their first public duties as a married couple during their honeymoon.

Camilla's Title's and Respect

Title

Camilla's title is the title of her husband that he had immediately at birth. After her marriage to Charles, Prince of Wales, Camilla became known as the Duchess of Cornwall and had several subsequent titles:

1. Her Royal Highness the Princess of Wales.
2. Rotseyskaya;
3. Duchess of Cornwall.
4. The Duchess of Chester.

Upon the death of Charles' mother Queen Elizabeth 2nd. The Prince of Wales became King Charles and Camilla the Duchess of Cornwall was titled Queen Consort.

Honours and Awards

Camilla, while Duchess of Cornwall, was awarded the following awards.

- Dame Grand Cross of the Royal Victorian Order (2012);
- Diamond Jubilee Medal of Queen Elizabeth II (2012) and others.
- Royal Lady of the Garter (2022)

Camilla's Public Life, Charities, and Patronage

Before the death of the Duke of Edinburgh and then Queen ElElizabethhe 2nd. Camilla was automatically ranked as the second-highest woman in the British order of precedence (after the Queen) and as the fifth or sixth in the order of precedence of her other kingdoms, after the Queen and the Duke. Two years after the wedding, the Queen gave Camilla visible signs of royal family membership by lending her the

Greville Tiara, formerly owned by the Queen Mother, and awarding her the Order of the Royal Family of Elizabeth II.

After their marriage, Clarence House became the Duchess and Prince of Wales's official residence. For Christmas events, the couple also stays at Birkhall, and for family gatherings, they stay at Highgrove House in Gloucestershire. They settled in Llwynywermod, Wales, in 2008, which they visit yearly every summer and at other times. The Duchess still maintains her Ray Mill House, where she lived from 1995 to 2003, to spend time alone with her children and grandchildren. Amanda MacManus, the Duchess of Cornwall's chief maid of honor, and her deputy private secretary were her bridesmaids at her wedding to Charles.

Although details were not public, Camilla's hysterectomy was confirmed in March 2007. She broke her left leg while walking up a hill in Scotland in April 2010. The Duchess and her husband were indirectly involved in the 2010 British student protests when protesters attacked their car in November 2010. Later, Clarence House issued a statement saying, "Protesters attacked a car carrying Prince Charles and the Duchess of Cornwall, but the couple was unharmed." The Queen designated the Duchess to the Royal Victorian Order on April 9, 2012, the 7th wedding anniversary of the Duchess and the Prince of Wales. The Prince of Wales commissioned a pub in Poundbury's village named after the Duchess in 2015. The Duchess of Cornwall Inn first opened its doors in 2016. The Queen appointed the Duchess to Her Majesty's Most Honorable Privy Council on June 9, 2016.

National And International Travel

Camilla's (the Duchess of Cornwall) first solo engagement was a visit to Southampton General Hospital; in June 2005, she attended the Trooping of the Color for the first time, making an appearance on Buckingham Palace's balcony. In November 2005, the Duchess visited the United States and met with President George W. Bush and First Lady Laura Bush at the White House as part of her inaugural tour. She then went to New Orleans to see the after-effects of Hurricane Katrina and met some residents whose lives had been drastically altered by the storm. The couple traveled to Egypt, Saudi Arabia, and India in March 2006. She presided over the naming ceremonies for HMS Astute and Cunard's new cruise ship, MS Queen Victoria, in 2007. The Duchess accompanied the Prince of Wales on a four-day tour of Turkey in November 2007. She and the Prince of Wales traveled to the Caribbean, Japan, Brunei, and Indonesia in 2008. They toured Chile, Brazil, Ecuador, Italy, and Germany in 2009. During her visit to the Holy See in

Italy, she met with Pope Benedict XVI. They later went to Canada. They traveled to Hungary, the Czech Republic, and Poland in early 2010. Camilla could not complete her engagements on her Eastern European tour due to a trapped nerve in her back. She accompanied the Prince of Wales to Delhi, India, to kick off the 2010 Commonwealth Games.

In March 2011, the Duchess and Prince of Wales paid visits to the heads of state of Portugal, Spain, and Morocco. The Duchess of Cambridge represented the British royal family at the 125th Wimbledon Tennis Championships in Wimbledon in June 2011. In the aftermath of the London riots, the Duchess followed the Prince of Wales to Tottenham in August 2011. The couple returned to Tottenham in February 2012, meeting with local shop owners six months after the riots to check in on them. On September 11, 2011, the Duchess joined the Prince of Wales and Prime Minister David Cameron at the 10th-anniversary memorial service for September 11, 2001, attacks in New York. In November 2011, the Duchess accompanied the Prince of Wales on a tour of the Commonwealth and the Persian Gulf Arab States. They visited South Africa and Tanzania, where they met with Presidents Jacob Zuma and Jakaya Kikwete.

The Duchess and Prince of Wales traveled to Norway, Sweden, and Denmark in March 2012 to commemorate the Queen's Diamond Jubilee. As part of the jubilee celebrations, the royal couple visited Canada for four days in May 2012. The Duchess of Cornwall and the Prince of Wales embarked on a two-week jubilee tour of Australia, New Zealand, and Papua New Guinea in November 2012. During their tour of Australia, they went to the 2012

Melbourne Cup, where the Duchess presented the race's winner with the Melbourne Cup. They visited Jordan in 2013 and met King Abdullah II and Queen Rania. They also visited Syrian refugee camps in Jordan. In May 2013, the Duchess went to the State Opening of Parliament for the first time, and the following month, she traveled to Paris on her first solo trip outside the United Kingdom. That same year, she attended the enthronement of King Willem-Alexander and Queen Máxima of the Netherlands and the preceding Queen Beatrix celebrations.

The Duchess and Prince of Wales attended the D-Day 70th-anniversary celebrations in Normandy, France, in June 2014 and they went on a nine-day tour of Mexico and Colombia in November of that year. The Duchess and Prince of Wales visited Northern Ireland and made their 1st joint trip to the Republic of Ireland in May 2015. The couple visited Australia in April 2018 and attended the opening ceremony of the 2018 Commonwealth Games. In November 2018, they also visited the West African countries of Gambia, Ghana, and Nigeria. The Prince of Wales and the Duchess of Cornwall went to Cuba on an official tour in March 2019, becoming the first British royals to do so; the tour was to strengthen ties between the United Kingdom and Cuba. The couple made their first official visit abroad since the start of the COVID-19 pandemic in March 2021, when they traveled to Greece at the invitation of the Greek government to commemorate the bicentennial of Greek independence.

Sponsorships

The Duchess supports several organizations, including St Catherine's School in Bramley, Animal Care Trust, The group of Chiropodists and Podiatrists, British Horse-riding

Federation, Dundurn Castle, Youth Action Wiltshire, New Queen's Hall Orchestra, London Chamber Orchestra, Elmhurst School for Dance, Trinity Hospice, St John's Smith Square, Georgian Theatre Royal. Arthritis The Duchess also sponsors the PG Wodehouse Society of the Netherlands, a non-British organization.

She is the Royal Navy Medical Service's honorary Commodore-in-Chief. In this capacity, she paid a visit to the training ship HMS Excellent in January 2012 to present medals to naval medical teams returning from Afghanistan. The Duchess is an honorary member of many additional patronages and was appointed a Gray's Inn judge in February 2012. In February 2013, she was named Chancellor of the University of Aberdeen, a ceremonial role that entails giving degrees to graduates, and she came to office in June 2013. She is the University of Aberdeen's first Chancellor and the only royal family member to occupy the office since it was established in 1860. In 2015, she was appointed head of WOW (Event of Women of the World), an annual festival commemorating women's and girls' achievements and examining the barriers they confront throughout the world, notably domestic abuse. In 2018 and 2020, she was named Vice Patron of the Royal Commonwealth Society and the Royal Academy of Dance, both of which the Queen was a Patron.

Osteoporosis Occurrence

After her mother died of osteoporosis that year, the Duchess became a member of the National Osteoporosis Society in 1994. Her maternal grandmother also died of the disease in 1986. She became a charity patron in 1997 and was appointed president in 2001 at a highly publicized event, accompanied by the Prince of Wales. In 2002, she released a mini book, A Skeleton Guide to a Healthy you, Vitamins and Minerals, to help women protect themselves from disease. The following month, she attended the International Women's Leaders Roundtable conference to Examine Barriers to Reimbursement for Osteoporosis Diagnosis and Treatment along with 13 eminent women worldwide. The International Osteoporosis Foundation organized the event hosted by Queen Rania of Jordan, and she delivered her first public speech during the event. The international conference in Lisbon, Portugal, brought together public figures from around the world to focus on the treatment of osteoporosis and called for government help worldwide. In 2004, she attended another Dublin conference organized by the Irish Osteoporosis Society. The following year, she traveled to Maryland to give a presentation on osteoporosis to high-profile health figures at the National Institutes of Health.

The Duchess of Cambridge launched the Big Bone Walk campaign in 2006, leading 90 children and people with osteoporosis to walk and climb across Loch Muick on the Balmoral Estate in Scotland to raise money for the charity. The campaign raised £200,000 and is now an annual fundraiser for the charity. In 2011, she played herself in the BBC Radio drama The Archers to raise awareness of the disease, and in 2013, she collaborated with the television show Strictly Come Dancing to raise funds for the Society. National Osteoporosis Day. By 2006, she had spoken at over 60 events about the disease in the UK and around the world and opened bone scanning units and osteoporosis centers to assist those affected. The Duchess participates in World Osteoporosis Day almost every year, attending events across the UK on October 20. She goes on to attend conferences worldwide and meet with health experts to learn more about the disease.

The Duchess received the Ethel LeFrak Award from an American charity in 2005 for her work raising awareness of osteoporosis worldwide and the Kohn Foundation Award from the National Osteoporosis Society in 2007. The Duchess of Cornwall Osteoporosis Center opened at the Royal Cornwall Hospital in Truro in July 2007. The same year, King's College London bestowed upon her an honorary fellowship for her efforts in raising awareness of osteoporosis. The National Osteoporosis Society established the Duchess of Cornwall Award in 2009 to honor her achievements in the field of osteoporosis. She was awarded an honorary doctorate by the University of Southampton in 2016. The National Osteoporosis Society was renamed the Royal Osteoporosis Society in 2019.

Fighting Against Rape and Sexual Abuse

After visiting nine rape crisis centers in 2009 and hearing survivors' stories, the Duchess began raising awareness and advocating for ways to help rape and sexual assault victims overcome and overcome their trauma. "The stories that Her Royal Highness heard on her first visit and the stories that she heard later left her with a strong desire to raise awareness of rape and sexual abuse and try to help those affected," according to The Times. " She frequently speaks with victims at a rape crisis center in Croydon and travels throughout the UK and abroad to meet with staff and victims at other centers. Boris Johnson, the Mayor of London, opened a rape victim center in Ealing, west London, in 2010. Hillingdon, Fulham, Hounslow, and

Hammersmith were where the center expanded. The Duchess of Cambridge established the Oakwood Place Essex Sexual Assault Referral Center at Brentwood Community Hospital in Essex in 2011.

In 2013, she convened a meeting at Clarence House for rape victims and rape support groups. Keir Starmer, the Director of Public Prosecutions, and Theresa May, the Home Secretary, were invited to the event. On several occasions, she presented a plan to assist victims: 750 toiletry bags filled with luxury toiletries were created by her Clarence House staff and distributed to victims at the centers. The Duchess was inspired to make the gesture after visiting a center in Derbyshire and asking victims what they needed to feel at ease following trauma and forensic examinations. According to Clarence House, the event was the first gathering of high-profile figures to focus solely on rape and sexual abuse issues. The same year, the Duchess visited Northern Ireland and established The Rowan, a sexual assault and referral center at Antrim Area Hospital, the first in Northern Ireland to provide assistance and comfort to victims of sexual assault, rape, and sexual abuse. During her Royal Tour of Canada in May 2014, the Duchess met privately with two women who had fled violent homes and received long-term support and shelter from Alice House in Dartmouth, Nova Scotia. During a tour of the Western Balkans with her husband in March 2016, the Duchess visited UNICEF programs in Montenegro and spoke about child sexual abuse while being shown an exclusive preview of a new app designed to protect children from online sexual abuse. The following year, the Duchess collaborated with the Boots retail and pharmacy chain to create a line of toiletry bags that would be delivered to sexual assault referral centers across the United Kingdom.

Other Topics

The Duchess is an advocate for literacy because she is an avid reader. Camilla supports the National Literacy Trust and other literacy organizations. She frequently reads to young children in schools, libraries, and organizations. She also participates in literacy celebrations such as International Literacy Day and World Book Day.

She went to the Hay Festival in 2011 to support children's literacy, and while there, she contributed books to the Oxfam bookstore. She also contributed to the Evening Standard's literacy campaign that year. The Duchess has also launched and consistently continues to launch literacy campaigns and programs. During a speech for the National Literacy Trust in 2013, the Duchess stated, "I strongly believe in the significance of igniting a passion for reading in the next generation." I was fortunate to have a father who was a voracious reader and a gifted storyteller. In a world where the written word fights for our attention with many other demands, we need more literacy heroes to continue inspiring young people to discover the pleasure and power of reading for themselves." Camilla has supported the Queen's Commonwealth Essay Competition since its inception in 2014. The program, which encourages young writers from around the Commonwealth to produce essays on different themes, is administered by the Royal Commonwealth Society, and the Duchess hosts the competition each year. Camilla has participated in 500 Words, a BBC Radio 2 contest for children to write and share their stories since 2015, and was named an honorary judge in 2018. She launched the Reading Room online club in 2021 to connect and share the interests and projects of readers, writers, and literary communities.

The Duchess supports several animal welfare groups, including Battersea Dogs & Cats Home and Brooke Hospital for Animals. She regularly goes to different animal shelters to show her support and to check how the animals are treated. Camilla adopted a Jack Russell Terrier rescue puppy from Battersea Dogs and Cats Home in 2011, then another from the shelter in 2012. In addition, in 2012, she created two veterinary clinics for ill animals at the University of Bristol's School of Veterinary Science in Langford, Somerset. Camilla worked with Fortnum & Mason in 2015 to offer 250 jars of honey made by bees in her private garden in Wiltshire; the £20 bottles ran out in two weeks, and the revenues were donated to the organization Medical Detection Dogs, of which she is a patron. Since then, the Duchess has sent a limited edition of honey to Fortnum & Mason every year, with the revenues benefiting various charities.

The Duchess supports organizations that fight poverty and homelessness all over the world. She is the patron of Emmaus UK, and she visited the charity's work in Paris in 2013 during a solo trip there. She visits Emmaus communities across the UK every Christmas. In a similar vein, the Duchess strongly supports credit unions, which she describes as a "true force for change in the financial landscape; they serve the people, not profit," and "they provide a friendly financial community where members benefit from each other's advice, as well as savings accounts and loans." It also supports organizations and programs that promote healthy eating and fights female genital mutilation, the arts, and heritage.

Fashion and style
Since her marriage, the Duchess of Cornwall has developed her style, trying on outfits and ensembles from notable fashion designers. She is said to prefer "characteristic styles of tea and shirt dresses" and favors "nude, white, and navy tones" and "scoop necklines." She has also been praised for her jewelry collections. In 2018, Tatler named her to their list of Britain's Best Dressed People, praising her hat choices that have given "the millinery a good name."

Titles And Styles Now

Since her marriage to the Prince of Wales, Camilla has been styled as the wife of a royal peer. She is generally referred to as "Her Royal Highness the Duchess of Cornwall," as Duke of Cornwall is one of her husband's titles. In Scotland, she is known as "The Duchess of Rothesay," after one of her husband's Scottish titles. She also bears the title Countess of Chester. n 2021, her husband became the Duke of Edinburgh following his father's death.

Legally, Camilla is Princess of Wales but has adopted the feminine form of her husband's highest-classified subsidiary title, Duke of Cornwall, because the title of Princess of Wales was strongly associated with that title's previous holder, Diana. If Charles becomes King, the Duchess would legally and automatically become Queen consort by English common law. At their wedding in 2005, Clarence House announced that Camilla would take the style of princess consort rather than a Queen; however, there is no legal or historical precedence for such a title. "Princess Consort" reflects the style of Albert, Prince Consort, husband of Queen Victoria. In 2018, Clarence House removed Camilla's proposed title statement from its official website. Clarence House, however, stated in 2020 that Camilla's ambitions to adopt the Princess Consort title would not change.

What is a Queen Consort?

A Queen or King consort comes to the throne by marriage to the heir apparent Queen or King. That is, she receives her title for being the wife or husband of the monarch on duty. "It refers to the wife of a ruling King and does not have the same powers as a Queen, who is considered the head of state," according to BBC Mundo. The main function that it would have is to provide support to the King or Queen in their tasks during their government. However, unlike the monarch, it does not have specific functions or established obligations and responsibilities.

However, when occupying a new position in the kingdom, the Queen or King consort will have to assume an important role in the various political commitments, public acts, official events, trips, and others. This way, Camila Parker-Bowles will have various appearances with her husband. Also, in many cases, the Queen consort attends the acts the King cannot attend. In this way, she compliments the work of the monarch and assumes some of the responsibilities that belong to her husband. Two royal consorts stood out in the United Kingdom: Prince Albert, Prince Consort of Queen Victoria, and Philip of Edinburgh, King Consort, for almost 70 years, in the reign of Elizabeth II.

What does it mean to be Queen consort?

This noble title refers to the wife of a ruling King who does not have the same powers as a Queen, who is considered the head of state. According to BBC experts on the British monarchy, "Queen consorts do not share the political and military powers of the monarch. Suppose the sovereign holds a title other than the King. In that case, his wife is referred to with the female equivalent, such as 'Princess consort,' Empress consort' or 'Grand Duchess consort'". In that sense, they explain that, unlike a Queen consort, "the Queen who bears her title in her own right usually obtains it by having inherited it after the death of the previous monarch."

What Is the Difference Between a Queen and A Queen Consort?

A Queen usually inherits the crown and refers to the eldest daughter of the current monarch. This means that she will have this official title by right or blood. No one can replace her unless she abdicates the throne or dies before her father. On the contrary, the Queen consort can only reach the throne if she marries the heir. For example, we have the case of Camila Parker Bowles, now named Queen consort due to her marriage to Prince Charles, the eldest son of Queen Elizabeth II.

Who currently holds the title of Princess of Wales?
After the sad death of Elizabeth II, the previous title that previously belonged to Camila Parker Bowles was inherited by Kate Middleton, William's wife, and nephew of the current King Charles III.

What is the difference between being a Queen heiress and a Queen consort?

Monarchies have been perpetrated for centuries in many countries, such as the United Kingdom, Spain, Japan, and Thailand. Kings or Queens must marry and produce offspring to ensure the continuation, and in this way, many people who were not linked to the nobility managed to enter this system.

Consort refers to the spouse of a monarch, but this differs by gender and country: usually, a King's wife is called a Queen consort, but a Queen's husband is treated differently. The men accompanying a Queen are generally Princes in Spain and the United Kingdom, as with Nicolás de Amsberg and Prince Philip of Edinburgh, respectively. Consorts do not have the same power as Kings but are treated as Royal Highness or Majesty. Being the monarchs' spouses, they can influence some decisions, as happened to Queen Elizabeth II, who decided that her children not only have the surname Windsor but also bear that of her husband, Mountbatten.

Difference between being Queen heiress and Queen consort.

An heiress Queen refers to the eldest daughter of the current monarch; therefore, she will be Queen by right or by blood. No one can take that place away from her unless she cannot perform her duties, abdicates the throne, or predeceases her father. Such was the case for Queen Elizabeth II: she was born the eldest child of King George VI and his wife, Elizabeth Bowes Lyon, and thus came to the throne as heir Queen. The Netherlands had three heirs to Queens for 123 years, Wilhelmina, Juliana, and Beatrix, with the latter giving birth to Willem-Alexander as her eldest son, the current King.

On the other hand, the Queen consort will only come to the throne if she marries an heir to the throne or heir-to-be. Camilla Parker Bowles will be Queen consort for her marriage to Prince Charles, eldest son of Queen Elizabeth II, and Kate Middleton will also be Queen consort for marrying Prince William, eldest son of Charles and Lady Di. Currently, there are more men on the throne by inheritance, which is why there are many Queen consorts. Some of them are Letizia from Spain; Maxim of the Netherlands; Charlene of

Monaco (although it is a Principality); Matilda of Belgium; and Rania from Jordan, among others.

Camilla Parker Bowles Is the New Queen Consort, As Elizabeth Wanted

Following the death of Queen Elizabeth II, Charles of Wales became the new Crown King of the United Kingdom, making his wife Camilla Parker the Queen Consort.

A spokesperson in March 2020 told The Times that they created the consort title so that when the Duchess accedes to the throne, she will become the Queen consort. "The intention is that the duchess will be known as the princess consort when the prince accedes to the throne," she clarified and clarified: "This was announced at the time of the wedding, and there has been no change." Let us remember that before the couple joined their lives in marriage, the Royal House announced the creation of this title: "The intention is that Mrs. Parker Bowles will use the title of HRH the Princess Consort when the Prince of Wales accedes to the Throne."

"It's a new title created just for Camilla because crowning her Queen would create public relations problems for the royals," columnist Daniel Engber wrote in February 2005.

It has always aroused mixed feelings among the subjects of Her Majesty Camilla Parker Bowles, 75, second wife of Prince Charles, now finally King. A woman who has been able to fight behind the scenes, struggling for years to break the barrier of distrust of the media and that part of public opinion that has remained linked to the memory of Lady Diana, a still very popular icon, who hated her for her proximity to the Prince of Wales and that in her he saw the ruin of her family. And finally managed to conquer even the sovereign Elizabeth, who only recently promoted her to Queen Consort when her son Charles would become King.

Charles and Camilla met in the 1970s. Camilla, one year older than Charles, surprised him by reminding him that one of her great-grandmothers, Alice Keppel, had been the lover of his great-grandfather, King Edward VII. The prince was then 22 years old; he courted her for six months but left for an internship in the Navy without the courage to take the decisive step and ask her for her hand. Camilla then took over the reins of her life, and she married a handsome officer, Andrew Parker Bowles, with whom she had two children, Tom and Laura Parker Bowles. A wedding that, for Charles, was a blow to the heart. As the chronicles of the main observers of the Royal House tell, only then did Charles realize how much he loved her. This a retrospective revelation, perhaps also due to the climate of distrust that once ran through Buckingham Palace towards Camilla, who was considered at the Palace as a 'girl with a past,' that is, no longer a virgin. Distrust did not discourage the two from building a clandestine relationship, making Camilla the prince's lover, who has always considered her the woman in his life, the only one capable of really understanding him.

But it is with the death of the 'princess of the people that the perspective around Camilla changes decisively, also thanks to a restyling of her look following her divorce and finally the wedding with the prince that consecrates her image as a woman capable of being next to the heir to the throne. Without ever making a blunder or letting one sentence slip, gracefully embodying the model of a stable woman, and carving out a decisive role for the family, as requested by Queen Elizabeth 2nd. Over the years, she has also brought her husband closer to her two children, William, and Harry, after the stormy period following Diana's death.

The Controversy Over a Possible Appointment

For a long time, it was rumored that Camila would not be named Queen consort if the current King Charles took the position. However, the doubts were cleared by Elizabeth II in an interview with The Mirror.

"When my son Charles becomes King, I know they will offer him and his wife Camilla the same support that they have given me, and it is my sincere intention that, when that time comes, Camilla be recognized as Queen consort while continuing her devoted duty," stated the late Elizabeth II.

What Functions Will Camilla Parker Bowles Perform as Queen Consort?

Before she died, Queen Elizabeth II expressed her desire for Camilla Parker-Bowles to become the Queen consort by proclaiming Charles of Wales, heir to the throne, as King. Under the name of Charles III, the son of the late Queen is now monarch of the United Kingdom, and his partner will accompany him in the role of consort. What does this title mean, and what functions should it fulfill?

Regarding the new title granted to Camila Parker-Bowles, we have shown you that this is a position that has existed in several kingdoms of the United Kingdom and that, for a long time, it was uncertain if Camila would carry it.

She becomes Queen Indirectly but without royal powers.
As previously stated, Camilla, Duchess of Cornwall, will be recognized as Queen Consort, a title bestowed upon her by Queen Elizabeth II after years of ambiguity going back to before her marriage to Prince Charles. Although a monarch's wife is traditionally crowned Queen, Camilla's title before Charles became King has long been debated. This is due to the sensitivity of her second wife's position and the flood of sadness that flowed over Britain after his first wife, Princess Diana, died in a car accident in 1997.

Charles and the Royal House have acted gingerly in this case, conscious of the popular impression of Camila as the "third person" who damaged Charles and the adored Princess Diana's marriage. On the other hand, Camila has won over many British people over the years with her prudence, down-to-earth manner, and devotion to her husband.

Camilla married Charles in a low-key civil wedding in 2005, becoming the new Princess of Wales, Diana's title, but calling herself the Duchess of Cornwall. Camila "wanted" to be identified as the "princess consort" rather than the conventional "Queen consort" when Charles ascended to the throne, palace officials have claimed for years. There is no precedence for the title of princess consort, as recommended by royal authorities. The term "prince consort" has only been used once: for Prince Albert, Queen Victoria's husband, from 1837 until 1901.

In 2010, NBC asked Charles whether Camilla would become "Queen of England, if and when you become King," to which he replied, "Well... We'll see, won't we?"

It's possible." When Elizabeth announced that she intended Camilla to be recognized as Queen consort once her son became King, the matter was resolved, an endorsement that formally represented the royal family's acceptance of Camila as a respected member and was widely interpreted as Elizabeth's move to ease the transition to Charles' reign.

"When my son Charles becomes King, I know they will offer him and his wife, Camila, the same support that they have given me; and it is my sincere intention that, when that time comes, Camilla will be recognized as Queen consort while she continues her devoted duty," Elizabeth said in February 2022, marking her 70th year in power.

Charles and Camila were "very mindful of honor," according to Charles.

"As we have worked together to serve and assist Her Majesty and the people of our areas, my loving wife has always been my staunch supporter," he added. Queen Elizabeth, George VI's wife, was the most recent Queen consort in British history, becoming known as the Queen Mother once her daughter became monarch in 1952.

Camila will be anointed during Charles' coronation, as is customary, although this might be skipped. Camilla Rosemary Shand is from an aristocratic family with long and deep links to the British royal family.

Camila married her longtime lover, Army soldier Andrew Parker Bowles, in 1973 while he was away. The couple split in 1995, soon after Charles confessed to having an affair with Camila in an explosive televised appearance. The next year, Charles and Diana divorced. Charles and Camila waited another nine years before marrying in a private ceremony at Windsor Guildhall in 2005. Camila has played hundreds of regal roles since then. She is a patron or president of more than 90 organizations specializing in animal welfare, literacy, and women's empowerment. She has also found her voice as a public speaker, receiving recognition for her work on sensitive issues such as sexual assault against women and domestic violence.

In 2021, she presented what many consider her groundbreaking address, calling "the males in our life" to become active in women's rights and offering condolences to the families of the women killed. Camilla's status as a high-ranking royal was reinforced the same year when Buckingham Palace named her a Royal Dame of the Noblest Order of the Garter, Britain's highest-ranking chivalry.

Fascinating Acts and Words Said by Camilla (Duchess of Cornwall) in the Public

1. "I'm Going to Self-Isolate."

In 2020, Camilla joked in her last public appearance with that curious phrase. If we look at the context, we understand everything a little better. It was during the visit of Prince Charles and Camilla to the British Museum of Transport, located in the heart of London. At one point in the tour, Parker starred in this unusual (and funny) moment: she got inside a bomb shelter and released the witty phrase. Logically, no one could contain their laughter, not even her husband.

2. Love for Animals

Camilla celebrated her birthday in 2019 surrounded by donkeys, but it is not the only time we have seen her very affectionate with animals. The Duchess is a huge animal lover, and when she comes across a dog or any other kind, she can't help but pet it. During her last trip to Australia with Prince Charles, she even held a koala in her arms. The Duchess was thrilled with the baby koala on her lap.

3. Traditional Dances as Well?

The adversity to airplanes is not an insurmountable barrier that prevents Camilla from traveling the world. As a crown representative, the duchess has certain obligations she must fulfill. And when she does, she gets involved to the fullest. So, on the official trip to Greece in May 2018, Camilla joined the Greek dancers as one more (except that she was not wearing a typical costume) and was encouraged to dance the sirtaki, one of the country's traditional dances. It all happened in the town of Acharnes, located on the island of Crete.

4. Beach Experience

Walking barefoot on the beach is a pleasant activity for anyone. The situation changes, however, when you are a member of royalty. But how can you resist if you find yourself on a paradise island with a beach of fine white sand? The Duchess of Cornwall took off her shoes to enjoy that pleasant feeling under her feet. Charles, the son of the Queen of England preferred to keep the shoes for the beach walk. Every man for himself. Natural above all.

5. Falling for The Smell of Flowers

When the Duchess of Cornwall does something, she does it from the heart. Therefore, in June 2018, she surprised the woman who gave her a bouquet by getting inside them. On that visit to the Garden Museum in London, Camilla was also paralyzed by a portrait of Prince Charles that was shown to her; we do not know if it was out of disgust or admiration for him. A complete visit and a little out of the ordinary.

6. A Bit of Ping Pong

Table tennis was one of Camilla's hidden hobbies that we didn't know about. In 2019, during the centenary celebrations of the Halton station of the Royal Air Force of Great Britain, Camilla opted during this celebration: to play ping pong. She was so excited that it was impossible to look away from her.

7. New Zealand Kisses

A few months ago, Camilla of Cornwall and Charles of Wales traveled to New Zealand. During the journey, they had the opportunity to integrate with the population and get closer to their culture.

8. Skin Games

Camilla seems to rub off on Charles, or their personalities are very similar. The couple complements each other well; for example, in this masquerade party, they held in their own home, Clarence House, in 2019. The reason for the celebration was to support elephant conservation. The ball was called the Dance of the Animals. It is a charity created by the Prince of Wales and the Duchess of Cornwall in 2016 dedicated to protecting African animals such as elephants, lions, and gorillas. Thanks to Selfridges and other firms from the fashion world, the organization has already raised more than 1.7 million pounds. The first dance was held in 2016 and was repeated in 2019. The last time, Camilla and Charles did not hesitate to pose with their bear masks?... Hopefully, they will repeat it.

Camilla's Hobby

Camilla admits that her secret hobby is Wordle. The Duchess of Cornwall gave an interview to Vogue in which she confesses that she plays the online word game Wordle with one of her granddaughters. Wordle is Camilla's most secret hobby.

Camilla has become a loved and respected person in a family where she did not get off on the right foot. The Duchess of Cornwall is very affectionate and smiles when she talks about her grandchildren, for example. She confessed that with one of her granddaughters, she plays a fun online word game called Wordle. She practices it every day with her. "She texts me to say: I've done it in three. And I tell him: I'm sorry, I've done it in two today", she says jokingly.

It is not the only secret that Camilla confessed during the interview. She acknowledges that beyond her extensive public work, representing the crown in numerous solidarity actions, the Duchess of Cornwall makes other regular visits in a private capacity. Very much in tune with what Prince William is used to doing, Camilla visits shelters in South London to talk to men and women in complex situations. She is known for her solidarity work which supports movements for women who have been victims of gender violence.

King Charles III and Camilla's Pet in the Buckingham Palace

Instead, King Charles III and Queen Consort Camilla have two rescue dogs, Beth, and Bluebell, both Jack Russell terriers. According to the British press, they will be the palace's first rescue dogs.

Their lives before the royal couple adopted them from Battersea Dogs and Cats Home in early 2017 are a long cry from the opulent royal estates they now enjoy. The two dogs were in pretty bad shape, according to Camilla's BBC Radio 5 Live report from 2020. Beth had been transferred "from pillar to post" before being abandoned. Bluebell was found "nearly dead" in the woods before she recovered, bald and covered with sores. Camilla told the radio listeners, "She's quite kind but, may we say, a touch neurotic."

Earlier this year, the two pups appeared on the cover of Country Life, adorned in the Duchess of Cornwall's pearls. The puppies were 11 (Beth, the black and white pup) and ten years old (Bluebell, the tan, and the white pup). They're very cute.

Camilla asked Britons to adopt pets from Battersea in July 2022, when the refuge was overwhelmed with animals. "You've all seen how simple it is to go there and come out with an animal; I've done it twice," she told the BBC. "Because of covid, many dogs and cats search for homes in Battersea. So, if I could persuade everyone listening and all your friends who want a dog or a cat to come to Battersea and create a lifetime companion, I would."

King Charles, who succeeded to the throne when his mother, Queen Elizabeth II, died, has always loved dogs, as did her mother. He has three Jack Russells (a separate breed from Parson Russell terriers in the UK) and a Labrador retriever Harvey, after the Winnie the Pooh character.

While Buckingham Palace is being renovated, the King and Queen Consort will live in Clarence House. We're sure Beth and Bluebell will enjoy sniffing about the area where the corgis and dorgis have resided for the last 70 years. Muick and Sandy, the Queen's last two Pembroke Welsh corgis, have gone to live with Prince Andrew and his ex-wife Sarah Ferguson.

Facts That Need to be Known So Far about Camilla, Queen Consort of the United Kingdom

1. She's a Little Carefree
Queen Camilla, aka Camilla Parker Bowles, was a down-to-earth country girl who won the British people's hearts with her natural, sincere demeanor - just as her current husband, King Charles, did 52 years ago. Despite being born into an upper-class family, Camilla never put on airs. "I have many friends who, if I even appear to be a little cocky, they'll just say, 'Look, come on, cheer up!' 'Don't be so damn grand!'" she said in a rare interview with the Daily Mail's "You" magazine. According to Vanity Fair, one former roommate described her bedroom as a shambles.

2. Her Engagement Ring Is Historically Significant.
A 5-carat emerald-cut diamond and three diamond baguettes are set into the gold engagement ring of Camilla Parker Bowles. This ring is not only beautiful, but it is also historically significant. The Queen's Ring was once owned

by the Queen, King Charles' grandmother. The Greville Crown, which the Queen Mother also passed down, is another royal jewel that Queen Camilla enjoys wearing.

3. Before Becoming Queen, She Held Numerous Titles.

Since Queen Elizabeth's death, Camilla has held the title of Queen Consort. Until then, however, she held several titles, each of which was complicated. When she married Charles, then Prince of Wales, she was bestowed the title of Duchess of Cornwall and the title of Her Royal Highness. She is also legally entitled to the title Princess of Wales, but she chose not to use it out of respect for Diana, the previous holder. Prince William's wife, Kate Middleton, has now been named Princess of Wales.

Camilla was known as the Duchess of Rossi in Scotland. She also received two foreign medals: the Star of Melanesia (Papua New Guinea) in 2012 and the Grand Cross (Canada) in 2014. (France). After Camilla's wedding, the Queen bestowed the Royal Coat of Arms on her. Camilla was also awarded the Royal Victorian Cross in 2012 and appointed to the Privy Council in 2016. Try saying it all at once.

4. She Likes Dogs

Queen Camilla adores her dogs in the same way that Queen Elizabeth adores her corgis. She adopted Beth, a Jack Russell terrier puppy, in 2011, the first puppy she ever rescued from a shelter. To keep Beth company, she adopted another dog, a Jack Russell named Bluebell, in 2012. The two are now the newest royal cubs at Buckingham Palace. Camilla also supports Charity Medical's testing dogs. She was able to observe dogs sniffing out various ailments. In

February 2019, she visited the puppies and their trainers and assisted in opening the new facility.

5 She Volunteers Extensively.

In addition to being a loving wife, mother, grandmother, and step-grandmother, Queen Consort Camilla gives generously to charity. She has become the patron or president of over 90 charities since marrying Charles in 2005. She supports charities supporting health and literacy, rape, sexual abuse, domestic violence victims, women's empowerment, food and animals, heritage, and the arts. Queen Elizabeth also left her some charities, including Barnardo's, Battersea Dogs & Cats Home, and The Royal School of Needlework.

6. She Is Well-Educated.

The Queen consort began her education at Dumbbells School in Sussex. She then attended Queen's Gate School in South Kensington before moving on to Mon Fertile School in Switzerland and the Institut Britannique in Paris.

7. She Enjoys Gardening.

Despite Camilla's numerous official responsibilities, "sometimes you get up in the morning and think you can't do it, and you just have to," she told a friend, according to the Daily Mail. "When you pause, it's like a balloon; you run out of puff and collapse in a heap." She maintains her country retreat, Raymill, where she can decompress and escape it. Camilla, like King Charles, has always enjoyed outdoor activities such as riding and hunting, and gardening is one of her hobbies. "If I could, I'd be out in my garden all day, every day," she once told reporters at an event for the

British charity Floral Angels. "I enjoy getting my hands dirty."

8. She's A Chatterbox.
Camilla's outgoing personality aids her success in royal life, even though she does not naturally crave the spotlight. The Queen consort credits her parents with teaching her manners and how to communicate with others, which she says makes royal duties easier. "I remember once there was a dinner party at home with some of the most boring neighbors in the world," she told the Daily Mail. "[My mother] would put us at the dinner table and, as soon as there was silence, she would say, 'Talk!'" I don't care what you talk about but keep the conversation going.' As a result, I've never been able to stop talking. It's in our nature not to be silent."

9. She Bursts Out Laughing.
Attending hundreds of engagements a year must be exhausting, and Camilla's sense of humor and sharp wit make it nearly impossible to keep a straight face, according to the Daily Mail. "You have to laugh through most things, and sometimes I laugh a little too much," she admits. "There are times when it's difficult not to lose it completely, especially when something goes wrong, and everyone stands there for a split second [unsure how to react]." To avoid laughing, you must swallow and pinch yourself very hard."

She appears to have this in common with her daughter-in-law Meghan Markle. Both women couldn't stop laughing when a buzzing bee broke up Prince Harry's speech at a May 2018 event. On the other hand, Camilla does not take herself too seriously: "You have to laugh at yourself because if you can't, you might as well give up!" she says.

10. She Is Terrified of Flying and Dislikes Traveling.

Despite her hectic schedule, Camilla is a homebody who dislikes traveling. She is afraid of flying. Her phobia prevented her from accompanying King Charles to several locations in Australia and the South Pacific (She did go to Brisbane, Australia, for the Commonwealth Games, but she declined the extra journey). Camilla, according to Express, uses EFT (Emotional Freedom Technique) tapping to help her cope with the stress of flying.

11. She Was Born on The Same Day as Former German Chancellor Angela Merkel.

They were born on the same day, July 17, seven years apart. Camilla celebrated her 70th birthday with an official portrait of herself relaxing in jeans in her garden, true to her easygoing style. A pair of parties were held to commemorate the occasion, one for her staff and charities and one for her family and friends.

12. She Wears the Same Chanel Shoes Every Time.

Could it be Chanel's double "C" logo, evocative of "Charles and Camilla," that draws her back to these cream pumps with black toes? (The logo is also said to be why Princess Diana never wore Chanel.) According to Footwear News, Camilla has been wearing the classic shoes since at least 2005, and they are no longer available for purchase.

13. She Is Related to Madonna, Celine Dion, and Charles!

Genealogical research has linked Queen Consort Camilla to famous pop stars Madonna, Celine Dion, and actress Angelina Jolie descended from the same 17th-century French Canadian couple.

Camilla and Charles share a genetic link, according to Ancestry.com, as they are both descended from Henry Cavendish, second Duke of Newcastle, making them ninth cousins once removed. In a scandalous twist, Camilla's great-grandmother, Alice Keppel, was the mistress of Charles's great-great-grandfather, King Edward VII. According to Ancestry, Charles and Camilla are half-second cousins once removed if Keppel's daughter Sonia (Camilla's grandmother) was the King's child.

14. She and Charles Had a Love-Hate Relationship.

The royal couple first met in the early 1970s, before Charles and Diana met. Despite their instant attraction, the Prince of Wales left for a tour of duty with the Royal Navy without declaring his intentions, and Camilla accepted a proposal from Army officer Andrew Parker Bowles, whom she married in 1973. "Everything in life is timing, and time so often deals you the wrong hand," Camilla's family friend Jane Churchill said of the couple to Vanity Fair.

15. Camilla Did Not End Charles' Marriage.

A devastated Charles was reportedly pressured into proposing to Diana by his father, Prince Philip. When asked if he and Diana were in love during a television interview, Diana replied, "Of course," but Charles cryptically added, "Whatever 'in love means."

It now appears that Charles and Diana were a bad match and that Charles had never moved on from Camilla.

However, when asked if he was faithful to Diana in a later interview, Charles replied, "Yes, until it became irretrievably broken down, us both having tried." Charles and Camilla were not free to appear in public as a couple until both of their marriages ended in the 1990s, after Diana's tragic death in 1997.

16. Camilla's Son's Godfather Is Charles.
Throughout Camilla and her husband's marriage, King Charles remained close friends. Charles was asked to be Tom's godfather when Camilla and Andrew's first child was born, and he agreed. However, Diana reportedly refused to include little Tom in their wedding party, despite Camilla and her son attending the ceremony. After Charles married Camilla, he became Tom's stepfather and godfather. Both Charles' and Camilla's children have stated that all they care about is their parents' happiness, and they have fond memories of their stepparents.

17. Her Brother Died in A Tragic Accident.
Mark Shand, Camilla Parker Bowles's brother, died suddenly in 2014 at 62 after falling and hitting his head outside a charity event in New York City. The tragic loss has left Charles and Camilla "utterly devastated," according to an official statement.

Camilla's parents also died, with her mother, Rosalind Shand, succumbing to osteoporosis in 1994 at 72. (Her grandmother had died of the same disease eight years before). "My family and I watched in horror as my mother shrank in front of our eyes," Camilla said, which motivated her to become president of the National Osteoporosis Society in the United Kingdom. Camilla's father, Major Bruce Shand, died in 2006 at 89, having witnessed his daughter marry Charles the previous year. Camilla maintains contact with her sister, Annabel Elliot.

18. Camilla Was Ill on the Day of Her Wedding to Charles.

According to Vanity Fair, Camilla was so sick with sinusitis on the day of her wedding, April 9, 2005, that she could barely move. She got out of bed when her sister, Annabel, threatened to put Camilla's wedding gown on. Because Charles and Camilla were divorced, they could not remarry in the Church of England, so they married in a civil ceremony followed by a church blessing at St. George's Chapel in Windsor Castle—the same location where Prince Harry and Meghan Markle later married.

Although Queen Elizabeth II was not always in favor of marriage, when it became clear that nothing could stop Charles from marrying his true love, she gave her approval. The Queen reportedly mentioned the Grand National horse race at the reception, saying, "They have overcome Becher's Brook and The Chair and all kinds of other terrible obstacles." They have delivered, and I am very proud of them and wish them well. My son is safe and sound at home with the woman he loves."

Her Sense of Humor

Camilla Parker Bowles has won Prince Charles over the years with her sense of humor. It has occupied the heart of Prince Charles of England for over three decades, but not that of the British people. After her adulterous relationship with the prince was discovered, she received numerous threats and even had 'brioches' thrown at her in a supermarket. Now, the inner circle of Camilla Parker Bowles has revealed in Vanity Fair magazine how she is the woman the Prince has been in love with all these years.

Many of us wonder how Charles of England fell in love with Camilla while still with the beautiful Diana. It seems Camilla's humour surpassed Diana's looks, according to a businessman friend of the Duke of Cornwall, Camilla has a sublime sense of humor and is very funny. The attitude contradicts that of Prince Charles, who has lived in a strict environment. A British aristocrat also agrees with this statement: "She is always in a good mood, she is tremendously funny, not at all snobbish, and she can even talk to walls."

Camilla's public image has changed since, in 2005, Diana of Wales revealed Camilla's relationship with her until-then husband. Today, the couple is fully accepted by the people. According to the statements for Vanity Fair by Nick Peto, a close friend of her first husband, Andrew Parker Bowles, Camilla has not changed in all these years, but the British people who had learned to love her have: "When they attacked her, she never complained. After all these years, no one can deny that she is a woman capable of making the prince happy."

In Vanity Fair, it is also said that Camilla had several partners before meeting the Prince. The best known was Andrew Parker Bowles, whom she married in 1973. Their wedding caused great sadness to Prince Charles, who did not lose hope until he finally asked for Camilla's hand. Those who once enjoyed the countryside, their horses, and their dogs today have a schedule full of events. But it hasn't always been that way. Camilla was not officially presented to the

Queen until 2000, and she was relegated to the background until she married the heir to the British crown in 2005.

SUMMARY

Charles and Camilla, their first love, is never forgotten. Shortly before Queen Elizabeth's death, they were still Prince of Wales and Duchess of Cornwall: now they are King Charles III and his Queen consort Camilla Parker Bowles. The love story of King Charles III and Queen Camilla was anything but conventional. Although he married Diana Spencer, Charles has never forgotten his ex-girlfriend, and, against all odds, they had a happy ending 35 years after their first meeting, confirming what was and is a torturous and compelling love story.

They discovered they share a love of polo and the outdoors and a sense of humor. Camilla makes fun of her great-romance grandmothers with King Edward VII, claiming, "Your great-grandfather was my great-grandmother's lover. I believe we have certain interests." They begin dating, but Charles must depart for eight months to serve in the Royal Navy. Camilla is engaged to someone else when he returns.

In July 1973, Camilla married Andrew Parker Bowles, an army cavalry officer who was seven years older than her and had formerly dated Prince Charles's sister, Princess Anne. They continue to have two children, Tom and Laura Parker Bowles. Charles and Camilla are still friends; in fact, Prince Charles becomes Tom's godfather.

On July 29, with around 750 million people watching around the world, and with Camilla present, Charles marries Diana in St. Paul's Cathedral. The two later have two children, Prince William, born in 1982, and Prince Harry, born in 1984, but their relationship soon becomes difficult. In June 1992, Andrew Morton Diana's book was released: Her True

Story; the Princess of Wales had recorded multiple tapes for the freelance writer, and its release shocked the world, thanks to his explosive stories about Diana's jealousy of Charles's involvement with Camilla. The question of whether Charles could be King if he divorced and remarried arises: he would not be permitted a second marriage in the Church of England since the King is the secular head of the church under the limits of the time. In December of the same year, Prime Minister John Major announced that Charles and Diana had officially separated.

And in January of '95, Camilla and Andrew Parker Bowles announced they would divorce. That November, reporter Martin Bashir does a now infamous television interview with Diana in which he asks if Camilla was a factor in her marriage breakup. And she says sadly, " There were three of us in this marriage, so it was a bit crowded ." A subsequent investigation would have concluded that Diana's brother Earl Spencer was "tricked and tricked" by Bashir into arranging a meeting with the princess and that Bashir used misleading practices to obtain her consent to the interview. The BBC only apologized for this in 2021.

The divorce of Charles and Diana became final in 1996. Diana sadly dies in a vehicle accident in Paris the following year, just after Charles throws a party for Camilla's 50th birthday at her country residence. As the world mourns the loss of Diana, Charles and Diana's sisters go to Paris to carry Diana's body back to England. Following the tragedy, Charles presents his relationship with Camilla to the public. A wave of criticisms and judgments overwhelms Charles and Camilla. There are no neutral opinions: there are those who take their side in support of the so-called ' true love ' and those who paint them as two monsters who have made one of the most loved women in the world suffer. Many also suspect that Lady D.'s death was purposely provoked due to her uncomfortable position, while others think that her death was faked and that she is still alive. Therefore, hypotheses and opinions of all kinds flew around.

Thirty-five years after their initial meeting, Charles and Camilla confirmed their engagement in February 2005. They will marry in a civil ceremony on April 8 with Prince William as a witness. The Queen does not attend the wedding but does attend the reception. Camilla receives the title of Her Royal Highness, the Duchess of Cornwall, for Diana to continue to be the only princess of Wales.

The couple isolates themselves in Birkhall, their home on the Queen's Balmoral estate, amid the coronavirus pandemic. Charles tested positive for the virus but had a mild case and recovered quickly; the couple reunited after completing their respective quarantines. The pair tweets a snapshot of themselves outside Birkhall with their dogs, Bluebell and Beth, to commemorate their 15th wedding anniversary. Charles will subsequently become ill again with Covid in 2022. In 2022, as part of a statement for her Platinum Jubilee, the Queen surprised fans by stating that it is her "sincere wish" that Camilla is acknowledged as Queen Consort when Charles ascends the throne. According to a Clarence House official, the Prince and Duchess are "moved and humbled by her Majesty's remarks." The pair then appeared on the Buckingham Palace balcony with the Queen at the last Platinum Jubilee ceremony.

After Queen Elizabeth's death and King Charles III's succession to the throne in September 2022, Queen Camilla's title became official. The royal family issued the following statement: "The Queen died peacefully in Balmoral this afternoon. The King and the Queen consort will stay at Balmoral tonight and return to London tomorrow. " Camilla was at her husband's side during mourning ceremonies for Queen Elizabeth and in the early days of King Charles III's reign. In the last few days, an old story returns to be heard, that of Simon Dorante-Day, who is convinced that he is the secret son of the new Kings of England. He has been asking for a DNA test for years. At the moment, however, it is considered only one of the many gossips related to the royal house. As well as the conspiracy theories about Lady D.'s death mentioned above.

Despite the whirlwind that overwhelmed Charles and Camilla due to their past, a new page in the history of the United Kingdom is now opening that arouses the interest of people from all over the world. *And it can certainly be said that the love of the two new rulers has overcome all kinds of obstacles and has been a winner.*

References and Citation

Camilla, Duchess of Cornwall - Alchetron, the free social encyclopedia. https://alchetron.com/Camilla,-Duchess-of-Cornwall

Camilla, Queen Consort - Wikipedia. https://en.wikipedia.org/wiki/Camilla,_Queen_Consort

Camilla, Duchess of Cornwall - INFOGALACTIC. https://infogalactic.com/info/Camilla,_Duchess_of_Cornwall

The Duchess: Camilla Parker Bowles and the Love Affair That Rocked the https://www.goodreads.com/book/show/35068600-the-duchess

Charles and Diana: A timeline of their relationship from first https://www.independent.co.uk/life-style/royal-family/the-crown-season-four-charles-diana-relationship-timeline-emma-corrin-b1393752.html

Prince Charles and the Duchess of Cornwall attend the Great Yorkshire .... https://www.dailymail.co.uk/femail/article-9791583/Prince-Charles-Duchess-Cornwall-attend-Great-Yorkshire-Harrogate.html.

Will Larry cope with Dilyn? Here's Battersea's advice on dogs and cats. https://inews.co.uk/inews-lifestyle/larry-dilyn-cat-dog-no-10-downing-street-battersea-advice-333724

Camilla is up close! The Duchess of Cornwall speaks exclusively. https://www.dailymail.co.uk/home/you/article-

4537074/Camilla-close-Duchess-Cornwall-speaks-exclusively.html

King Charles III arrives at the massive crowd outside Buckingham Palace ....
https://www.foxnews.com/entertainment/king-charles-iii-arrives-massive-crowd-outside-buckingham-palace-following-queen-elizabeths-death

19 Things You Didn't Know About Camilla, Queen Consort of the United https://www.msn.com/en-us/lifestyle/travel/19-things-you-didn-t-know-about-camilla-queen-consort-of-the-united-kingdom/ar-AAYa2wi

Queen Consort Camilla's health woes explained as she's in 'quite a lot ....
https://www.mirror.co.uk/news/health/queen-consort-camillas-health-woes-28007799.

Princess Diana - Biography - IMDb.
https://www.imdb.com/name/nm0697740/bio

19 things you didn't know about Camilla, Queen Consort of the United https://www.rdasia.com/culture/19-things-you-didnt-know-about-camilla-queen-consort-of-the-united-kingdom

Printed in Great Britain
by Amazon

35724195R00040